Contents

BASIC ORIENTATION • 1

THE PRE-VISIT STAGE • 5

Telephone Calls 7
 Routine Calls • Camouflaged Specialty Calls •
 The Answering Machine

Mail 15
 Unsolicited Guidance Material • "Teasers"

Gifts 18
 Great • Nice • Terrible

It's Time for a Visit 25
 Her Turf or Yours • The Eighty-Mile Umbilical
 Prerogative • Additional Reasons to Visit Your
 Mother

Making The Announcement 30
 No Surprises, Please!

Preparations 34
 Your Mother Prepares for The Visit • You
 Prepare for The Visit

More Gifts 38
 The Symbolic Token Gift • The Official Visit
 Gift

THE VISIT STAGE • 42

INITIAL CONTACT	43
Initial Visual Contact • The Ride to Your Mother's Home • What to Talk About • What to Avoid Talking About	
LANGUAGE USAGE	52
GETTING SETTLED	57
Doing-for-You • Presenting the Official Visit Gift	
DINNER	58
The Maternal Multiple • A Late-Night Snack	
THE FIRST MORNING	64
Bathroom Ground Rules • Interior Decoration	
PLANNING A DAY'S ACTIVITIES	67
Breakfast	
THE MALL	68
THE POOL	73
Reading Material • Wearing Apparel • Miscellaneous Advice	
DINING OUT	75
THE INEVITABLE BLOW-UP	78
THE DEPARTURE	84
Prolonging The Visit • The Goodbye	

THE POST-VISIT STAGE • 89

How to Visit Your Mother

The Official Survival Manual

For Children Ages 20 thru 60

Dennis Paget and Leonard Majzlin

Illustrations by Leonard Majzlin

ST. MARTIN'S PRESS • NEW YORK

Authors' Disclaimer

Though the authors have immediate family living in the Sun Belt, any similarity between members of their families and people, places, and situations depicted in this book is purely coincidental. (Our lawyer, who has a mother living in Florida, strongly recommended this paragraph; otherwise we might have our heads handed to us.)

Nevertheless, this book is affectionately dedicated to our parents
Charlotte and Jesse Paget
Freda and Gregory Majzlin
whose love inspired its creation.

HOW TO VISIT YOUR MOTHER. Copyright © 1986 by
Dennis Paget & Leonard Majzlin. All rights reserved.
Printed in the United States of America. No part of this
book may be used or reproduced in any manner
whatsoever without written permission except in the case
of brief quotations embodied in critical articles or
reviews. For information, address St. Martin's Press,
175 Fifth Avenue, New York, N.Y. 10010.

Design by M. Greenstien

Library of Congress Cataloging in Publication Data

Paget, Dennis.
    How to visit your mother.

    1. Mother and child—Anecdotes, facetiae, satire,
etc. I. Majzlin, Leonard. II. Title.
PN6231.M68P33   1986   818'.5402   85-25124
ISBN 0-312-39624-4 (pbk.)

First Edition
10 9 8 7 6 5 4 3 2 1

Basic Orientation

Once upon a time, life was much simpler. We lived in

NEIGHBORHOODS

A neighborhood was where your milk was delivered, diapers were delivered, and often babies were delivered, where doctors made house calls and no one made phone calls, they just opened the window and yelled or walked down the street and knocked on your door.

Everyone knew who you were.

You lived

AT HOME

And what your mother did at home was (among other things) to

BE A MOTHER

Every day and every night. From month to month and year to year.

She DID THINGS for you.

And it went on for a long time.

And there's one thing for sure when you do something for a long time:

YOU NEVER FORGET HOW TO DO IT

Today, you are an adult, living in an adult world, and chances are neither you nor your mother lives in the same city, let alone the same neighborhood in which you grew up.

This has created a new phenomenon. It's called

THE VISIT

And what happens when you get together with your mother either on the phone or under the same roof is that a whole flood of elusive, subtle feelings and memories come flowing in, affecting how you both behave.

THE VISIT

is what this book is all about. And everything that leads up to and flows from

THE VISIT

is what comprises your adult life with your mother.

4 · How to Visit Your Mother

Therefore, this manual is divided into three parts:

> THE PRE-VISIT STAGE
> THE VISIT STAGE
> THE POST-VISIT STAGE

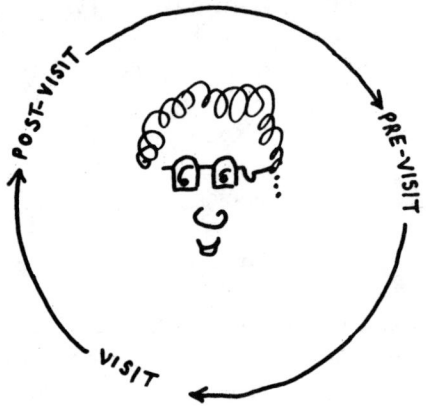

Keep in mind that throughout this entire manual, and at any given moment, your mother's life with you exists in one of these stages.

The Pre-Visit Stage

The PRE-VISIT STAGE is characterized by two facts of life:

1. You're not with her *right now.*
2. You haven't *just been* with her.

THIS MEANS ONLY ONE THING IN YOUR MOTHER'S MIND:

Be aware that most of your adult life with your mother takes place in THE PRE-VISIT STAGE.

Whether you know it or not, inherent here is a subtle strategy to bring you to a special moment:

ANNOUNCING YOUR FORTHCOMING VISIT

Hidden among ordinary DAY-TO-DAY INNOCENT EXCHANGES are subtle hints, designed to commit you to a definite date in time.

Therefore, it is imperative that you be aware of these DAY-TO-DAY INNOCENT EXCHANGES and be able to differentiate between innocent exchanges and the ones that will propel you closer and closer to THE ANNOUNCEMENT.

These exchanges appear in the form of telephone calls, mailings, and gifts.

Telephone Calls

There are two kinds of telephone calls between you and your mother:

ROUTINE CALLS

CAMOUFLAGED SPECIALTY CALLS

A ROUTINE CALL from your mother is nothing more than an expression of her desire to connect with you, even briefly, to let you know that she still loves you, and to

HEAR YOUR VOICE

Whether this occurs twice a day, twice a week, or twice a month, and no matter how ordinary the subject matter may be, she simply wants to

HEAR YOUR VOICE

Under normal circumstances, if you receive a routine phone call from a friend or someone selling dance lessons, and the time is not convenient for you to talk, you simply offer to return the call or ask if the person can call you back.

No problem.

However, your mother rarely calls when you are just reading a book or watching television.

A ROUTINE CALL from your mother is more likely to arrive when:

> the dog has just peed on the white couch
>
> your spouse has been working late at the office and you just found out why
>
> your teenage daughter just said she didn't think a girl could get pregnant from doing it once

the I.R.S. just told you how much you have to come up with in ten days

you've just been told your shrink has moved in with your lover

your mechanic just called with the estimate on how much it will cost you to replace the cylinder block in your car

your two-year-old just locked himself in the car and is sucking on your only key

your parakeet got loose and the cat has him cornered in the TV room

your son is taking a bath and a rubber duck has just floated into the living room

your son's gerbil just stopped breathing

you are totally absorbed in discovering a new erogenous zone

Receiving your mother's phone call under these circumstances creates a problem . . . because the minute your mother

HEARS YOUR VOICE

she will sense that something's up.

This is a result of the fact that she possesses

MOTHER-RADAR

10 · How to Visit Your Mother

Unlike conventional radar,

MOTHER-RADAR

detects what is *not* there. As a result, whether you decide to call her back or continue to have a conversation, two things will automatically happen.

SHE'LL BEGIN TO WORRY

SHE'LL THINK IT HAS SOMETHING TO DO WITH HER

We strongly advise that you not attempt to have a conversation if your mind is diverted; it will only confirm her conclusion. The more you try to assure her that everything's fine, the more she'll be convinced that everything's

NOT FINE

And if everything's NOT FINE, there's only one conclusion a genuine Mother-Who-Cares can draw:

IT MUST BE TIME FOR A VISIT

She will tuck this in the back of her mind and continue to carry on with normal telephonic "mini-visits." These will begin to take the form of CAMOUFLAGED SPECIALTY CALLS .

For example:
Your birthday is tomorrow but your mother's calling you today to find out where you'll be tomorrow so she can call you to wish you a happy birthday.

Research has indicated that in a CAMOUFLAGED SPECIALTY CALL the actual reason for calling will appear no earlier than thirteen and no later than fifteen minutes into the conversation . . . and will always be in the form of a . . .

SUBTLE HINT

The following are examples of SUBTLE HINTS that may appear in a

CAMOUFLAGED SPECIALTY CALL:

"I've been meaning to tell you . . .
I was speaking to your cousin Shirley and she said that her sister-in-law is moving to [your town] so I told her you'd know someone who could help her find an apartment."

"Listen . . .
I was sitting by the pool the other day and a friend of Mrs. Kolodny who lives upstairs happened to be telling her about the wonderful Caribbean cruise her children gave her for her birthday."

"Before I forget . . .
I just happened to be flipping through *Cosmo* the other day at the dentist's and came across this article that said people who are married live a lot longer than people who are not married."

"You want to hear something interesting?
I was at a luncheon with Pearl last Monday and she said that her husband, Sam, who used to be an accountant for W. T. Grant said it really pays to have children nowadays because of the new tax deductions the government gives you."

"I've been thinking . . .
I saw a commercial on television the other day for some kind of new telephone service and it said the more you use the telephone the less it'll cost you."

"By the way . . .
Do you know how long it's been since I've seen you?"

The following are recommended as POLITE TACTICAL RESPONSES with regard to these sensitive areas:

> "How interesting."
> "How nice."
> "I didn't know that."
> "So I've heard."
> "Really?"

You will notice that these TACTICAL RESPONSES are applicable in every case, except for the last question, "Do you know how long it's been since I've seen you?"

This is the ultimate CAMOUFLAGED SPECIALTY CALL because it is the vehicle your mother will use to initiate the process of bringing you closer to that special moment:

ANNOUNCING YOUR FORTHCOMING VISIT

Everything the Manual has stated with regard to telephone calls is admirably demonstrated when your mother comes into direct contact with a mechanical device with which she is uncomfortable and would just as soon do without:

THE TELEPHONE ANSWERING MACHINE

Our research has indicated only one type of reaction ever recorded on ANSWERING MACHINES whenever mothers have called.

> "(sigh) . . . (click)"

Although we have polled countless people regarding their mothers' attitudes concerning ANSWERING MACHINES, their mothers seem to have their OWN reasons for not wanting to leave a message on a machine.

Here are some of them:

> HOW DO I KNOW YOU'LL GET THE MESSAGE
>
> I NEVER KNOW WHAT TO SAY
>
> IT DIDN'T SOUND LIKE YOU
>
> IT MAY BE GOOD ENOUGH FOR YOUR CLIENTS, BUT NOT FOR ME
>
> I'M TOO OLD FOR THIS
>
> WHY SHOULD I HAVE TO SPEND THE MONEY IF YOU'RE NOT THERE
>
> WHY SHOULD OTHER PEOPLE KNOW OUR BUSINESS
>
> I DON'T LIKE ANYBODY TO TELL ME WHEN TO TALK
>
> I DON'T NEED TO CALL LONG-DISTANCE TO TALK TO MYSELF
>
> HOW DO YOU EXPECT ME TO TALK WHEN NO ONE'S LISTENING
>
> ANSWERING MACHINES ARE FOR *OTHER* PEOPLE, NOT MOTHERS

Mail

Around this time, you will notice that the volume of mail you receive from your mother may increase in two areas.

UNSOLICITED GUIDANCE MATERIAL and "TEASERS"

UNSOLICITED GUIDANCE MATERIAL often comes in the form of newspaper, magazine, and newsletter clippings, handbills, souvenir programs, and occasionally other people's letters and cards. They often have a personal notation written in the margin or a small note attached.

Here are some examples of UNSOLICITED GUIDANCE MATERIAL:

> a movie review of *Yentl* from the *Yorba Linda Shopping Mall Weekly*, written by someone named Candi Flanagan, with your mother's margin note saying, "She and I agree a hundred percent. Don't miss it!"

> the side of a Rice-a-Roni box, containing an exciting recipe for Rainbow Chicken, using maraschino cherries, broccoli, orange peel, and Nestle's Quik, with your mother's note attached saying, "I made this for my Canasta group and no one could guess what was in it!"

> a tear-off coupon she got while standing in a bus, which shows five undiscovered tax tips from H & R Block, and your mother's note attached saying, "Does your accountant know about this?"

> an article from the Indian River Shopping Mall Newsletter showing the best way to remove borscht stains from clothing, with your mother's note saying, "I wish I knew about this years ago."

> an article with the headline "Contemporary Viennese Psychiatrist's Book Debunks Freudian Theories," and your mother's

margin note saying, "I could have told them this years ago, if they'd only asked."

Mail in the form of

TEASERS

is often the best way your mother will begin to subtly hint that it's

TIME FOR A VISIT

Here are a few examples of TEASERS:

> a flyer from J. C. Penney announcing a colossal after-Christmas sale of designer clothing, with a note from your mother saying, "Even if I didn't live here, it would be worth your coming down."

> a handbill announcing that the Palmetto Playhouse will be presenting a star-studded production of *The Odd Couple* with Durward Kirby and Soupy Sales, and your mother's note attached saying, "I'm getting tickets for this and can't wait to see it! Wouldn't it be nice if you could join me?"

> a magazine ad indicating a half-price car rental given with an Eastern Airlines ticket to Florida if purchased within 60 days, with no note attached at all.

> a news article about a little boy who traveled by himself to Arizona to visit his grandmother and how well-treated he was by the airlines personnel, with your mother's margin note saying, "Isn't this a wonderful story?"

a magazine article on how a young person from Cleveland moved to her area last year, opened a little donut stand, and now owns five drive-in donut stands in her county alone, grossing over half a million dollars, with a note from your mother saying, "It's amazing what a young person with a good head on his shoulders can do here."

a weather map from the local newspaper indicating that the coldest winter the north has ever experienced is expected this season, with a notation from your mother saying, "I can't believe that the same day I went swimming I read this!"

a handbill for a four-day Office Management Seminar to be held in a Ramada Inn not far from your mother's home, with a note saying, "Sam, who used to be an accountant with W. T. Grant, says you could deduct the whole trip here from your taxes and all you'd have to do is sign-in the first morning."

Other things will be traveling back and forth through the mail:

Gifts

There are GREAT GIFTS, there are NICE GIFTS, and there are TERRIBLE GIFTS.

A GREAT GIFT is:

1. something your mother can really use
2. something your mother will not buy for herself
3. something your mother wouldn't expect

4. something your mother can use often, perhaps daily
5. something your mother can use around other people
6. something that evokes admiration and a reaction from her friends; in other words,

WILL IT PLAY AT THE POOL?

Based on these criteria, a gift to your mother of the Hope Diamond resting on a red velvet pillow, surrounded by a satin lining, in a sterling silver filigree box, is not really a GREAT GIFT. Although it is truly an exceptional item, she really hasn't got much use for it; if she knew you were in a position to actually BUY the Hope Diamond she'd *expect* that you might buy it for her; carrying it around on a daily basis could prove more of a burden than a blessing to her; since it has no function other than to just *be* ... it would be difficult to work into her routine conversation ("I know the Woolite coupons are in here somewhere—maybe under the Hope Diamond"); it would most certainly evoke a reaction from other people (probably your mother's only benefit from owning it).

On the other hand, an eye-catching, everyday watch, bracelet, or locket is a GREAT GIFT.

An attractive beach robe is a NICE GIFT. It could conceivably qualify as a GREAT GIFT only if you have already provided her with *others,* so she doesn't have to be seen wearing any one robe too often.

A NICE GIFT will often meet all of the criteria for a GREAT GIFT except for the first one. In other words, a GREAT gift is one she can . . .

REALLY USE

20 · How to Visit Your Mother

A NICE GIFT is one she can

ALWAYS USE

A box of lovely handkerchiefs is a NICE GIFT.

A TERRIBLE GIFT to your mother is one that may satisfy some of the aforementioned criteria, but that overall shows you have hardly any idea of her desires, needs, or taste.

Some examples of TERRIBLE GIFT IDEAS are:

Frederick's of Hollywood peek-a-boo underwear

a set of Nautilus equipment

a book entitled *Beginner's Guide to Cooking*

a string bikini

a roach holder (not to be confused with a Roach Motel, which you wouldn't get for her either)

a "Best of The Rolling Stones" album

a framed photo of you standing with your spouse and mother-in-law

a photograph of you on a nudist beach

a carton of bubble gum

one earring

a Chicago Cubs baseball jacket

an autographed first edition of *Portnoy's Complaint*

breakdance lessons

We also recommend sending unexpected gifts to your mother—even flowers—as often as possible. An unexpected gift can only serve to make her feel great . . . even though, upon receiving it, she will always say:

These same three categories hold true for gifts your mother may send to *you*.

Our research indicates that at one time or another you will get a gift from your mother that has no relevance whatsoever to your life, your needs, your taste, or your desires.

And you know it the moment you open the box because:

> it's the fourth terry cloth bathrobe you've received from her in three years
>
> it's a twenty-four-inch salami and you've been a vegetarian for five years
>
> it's a St. Laurent velour evening coat and you're into cutoff jeans

It is not inconceivable that one corner of the closet of the thin, balding secretary/treasurer of the Minnetonka Birdwatching Society is filled with the same stack of gifts as the closet of his burly, long-haired brother who is the lead drummer for the rock group Hostile Hubcaps.

This is your mother's way of not playing favorites.

Invariably, this gift was purchased in a store that has no branch in your town. So there's absolutely no way you can return it or get a credit . . . unless you visit your mother.

The phenomenon of gifts that miss the mark is one that can continue for decades . . . unless you decide to say something about it to your mother. However, a word to the wise . . . don't.

By now you have experienced various subtle pressures over a period of weeks or months and the thought is beginning to occur to you that

It's Time for a Visit

HER TURF OR YOURS

For the purposes of this manual, we are going to avoid discussing factors of expense, extreme distance, and how many children you may have, because even though you may live in Anchorage, Alaska, with your spouse and seven children all under the age of nine, and your travel budget can get you only as far as downtown Juneau and your mother lives in a small Winnebago camper just off a causeway in Fort Myers, Florida, she will always prefer to have you visit *her*, rather than the other way around.

Why?

In the past, most of the time that your mother spent with you was spent

AT HOME

And during that time, most of her waking moments were occupied with one thought:

TO DO-FOR-YOU

Whether it was to shop, to clean, to cook, to feed, to educate, or to clothe, it all came under the general activity

TO DO-FOR-YOU

Today, the optimum environment where your mother can best recreate this atmosphere, one in which she can continue to DO-FOR-YOU, is to be found only in her home. It is *never* in yours.

For example: if your mother comes to visit you and stays over, and walks into the kitchen the next morning to get a cup of coffee, chances are she's already made up her bed.

If you stay overnight at your *mother's* home, and you walk into the kitchen the next morning to get a cup of coffee, somehow, mysteriously, she manages to leave the kitchen, make up your bed, and return to the kitchen before your spoon is even in the cup.

The important distinction to make is that she will have done this even before making up her OWN bed.

What this means is that in her own home she is more comfortable

DOING-FOR-YOU

When was the last time your mother made up your bed in *your* home?

Chances are, never.

Unless, perhaps, if you are single.

Our research indicates that the only time your mother feels truly comfortable performing any activities in your home is when you are single, ill, or pregnant.

Otherwise, there are only two publicly sanctioned activities your mother performs in your home:

        1. Buying a dust ruffle

        2. Installing shelf paper

Of all the things your mother likes to DO-FOR-YOU, there is one that best symbolizes the homey atmosphere she would like to recreate and that is

FEEDING YOU

Feeding you was the first most important thing she ever did for you. And wherever and whenever possible she's going to do it again . . . and again . . . and again . . .

And the best place to do it is on HER OWN TURF because

> that's where *her* pots and pans are
>
> that's where *her* dishes and glasses are
>
> that's where *her* silverware is
>
> that's where everything she's cooked in, served on, or eaten from for decades is
>
> that's where she knows the butcher who'll always give her the best cut of brisket
>
> that's where she'll count on the man to tell her not to take the halibut but the flounder
>
> that's where with a wink she can get an extra peach thrown in
>
> that's where she has a hand-chopper and a wooden bowl, not a Cuisinart
>
> that's where she can do what she wants with leftovers
>
> that's where she knows what belongs in what bowl
>
> that's where she knows which drawer the potholders are in
>
> that's where she knows which can opener really works
>
> that's where they'll slice the smoked fish the way she knows you'll like it
>
> that's where she knows that the sugar is in the tea cannister, the tea is in the coffee cannister, and the coffee is in the freezer
>
> that's where her Pyrex measuring cup that used to have red numbers on it is

It should be very obvious by now that the objective of visiting your mother is to make both of you happy, and an atmosphere of peaceful coexistence is more easily created on her turf than on yours. In most cases, you and your family will have to work twice as hard to make your mother comfortable in your own home. Let us remind you that no matter how hospitable you are to her, no matter how many pillows you place on her bed, no matter how many fresh oranges you squeeze every morning or how nicely you arrange the sliced banana on the All-Bran, in her mind, she is not

A MOTHER

She is

A GUEST

And a guest doesn't DO-FOR-YOU. Being a good guest means accepting the fact that it is more blessed to receive than it is to give. Most people are pleased to be waited on hand and foot. To your mother, it means you don't want her in your kitchen. And no matter how hard she tries to help out, deep down where it really counts she always feels she's

IN THE WAY

How do you determine where you will stay?

You don't.

Just as nations establish territorial boundaries within twelve to two hundred miles from their shores, mothers have their own sovereign claims as well. This is known as . . .

THE EIGHTY-MILE UMBILICAL PREROGATIVE

It means that if you so much as set foot within an eighty-mile radius of your mother's house, and she knows about it, it is understood that you will most probably stay there.

Of course, if you and your seven children arrive at your mother's small Winnebago camper, it probably wouldn't make sense for all of you to crowd in.

But don't think for a minute your mother won't insist that some of the children stay with her anyway.

If all the subtle pressures and preceding rationale have not convinced you that THE VISIT should be on your mother's turf, the following list might provide you with some additional motivation.

ADDITIONAL REASONS TO VISIT YOUR MOTHER

your children's school vacation

your work vacation

the Super Bowl is in Los Angeles

there's a Marlin Tournament in Key West

spring training starts in Tucson with your favorite baseball team

you have a company sales meeting in New Orleans

your lover has a sales meeting in New Orleans

you have an uncontrollable urge for Joe's stone crabs in Miami the Bob Hope Golf Tournament in Pebble Beach

the Daytona 500 Auto Race

your son's doing a school report on the Cape Canaveral Space Center

while talking to your mother, she said she was thinking of changing her will

a snowstorm is predicted where you live

your boss's daughter's wedding is in Louisville

while talking to your mother, she said, "What's a codicil?"

your apartment is being painted

you received a set of golf clubs for Christmas

your doctor says you have a Vitamin D deficiency and need sun

while talking to your mother, she said, "What's an irrevocable trust?"

you can't get a reservation at the Dorado Beach Hotel in San Juan

your kids want to go to Disneyland

your mother asks if it's possible to fire an executor

your daughter wants to get engaged to a Cherokee Indian and she'd like you to meet his parents on their reservation

you'd like to shake down your new cabin cruiser on the inland waterway

your mother says she didn't think you'd mind it if your

brother-in-law was her executor

your spouse books into the same spa for the fifth time with "a friend" and you're suspicious

It is obvious that if one or more of these reasons apply, they may also determine WHEN you will visit and FOR HOW LONG. The length of a VISIT is of utmost concern to your mother and the members of her community. This concern is best expressed by the time-honored and revered Golden Maxim

**NO MATTER HOW LONG THE VISIT
IT'S NEVER LONG ENOUGH**

It seems the time has now arrived for

Making The Announcement

FIRST AND FOREMOST: DO NOT TELEPHONE YOUR MOTHER UNTIL YOU HAVE DEFINITE CONFIRMATION OF AIRLINE SPACE. The reasons for this are that (a) many activities are set in motion once the ANNOUNCEMENT is officially made and (b) there is one element you must never, ever be responsible for introducing in a VISIT to your mother or you will live to regret it, and that is the element of

SURPRISE

Now, you may not *mind* surprises.

In fact, you may even *like* surprises.

But one thing's for sure:

YOUR MOTHER HATES SURPRISES

And the reason she hates surprises is that they catch her off guard. To your mother, there is nothing worse than being caught off guard—because to be caught off guard is to be

UNPREPARED

From the moment you MAKE THE ANNOUNCEMENT to the beginning of THE VISIT STAGE, your objective is to make sure that your mother

KNOWS WHAT'S COMING

For example, when your mother first greets you at the beginning of THE VISIT, and she can't seem to take her eyes off your daughter, you might think that it's because of your daughter's pink hair . . .

or perhaps it's because your daughter's sneakers are so worn through that her toes are peeking out . . .

or perhaps your mother's bothered by the fact that your daughter is also wearing a nun's habit.

But it's not these observations per se that are bothering her. What's REALLY bothering your mother is that

NO ONE TOLD HER AHEAD OF TIME

This is not necessarily your fault or even the result of a lack of communication. Things you've learned to take for granted may take on much greater importance from her point of view. What's worse, non-disclosure of information has a significance all its own. This is because your mother still adheres to an age-old belief:

FROM A MOTHER YOU DON'T KEEP SECRETS

It is in your best interest, therefore, during this stage, to prepare your mother for anything that may be unexpected.

Between now and the time of your VISIT, via CAMOUFLAGED SPECIALTY CALLS or letters, tell her as much as you possibly can, to avoid problems later on.

Our research indicates that during the days or weeks following THE ANNOUNCEMENT, your mother will check your flight information with you many times, until you actually depart for THE VISIT. She does this for the following two reasons:

> *It's almost too good to be true*
>
> *It's her way of asking, "Are you still coming?"*

Because of this repetition of your flight information, there is a strong possibility that confusion may occur. Consider, for the moment, these flight numbers and arrival times:

FLIGHT #359	arriving at	1:10
FLIGHT #220	arriving at	12:30

This may appear simple, but it isn't. Take the first flight, #359, which arrives at 1:10, for example. As a result of your mother's ANTICIPATION about your arrival and the constant repetition of the numbers in your flight information, there is a good possibility that she may, instead, show up at the airport at 3:59, hoping to meet Flight 110. Therefore,

YOU DO NOT WANT FLIGHT NUMBERS THAT SOUND LIKE ARRIVAL TIMES

We strongly advise that you call her the day before you actually leave, to clarify once again the arrival details—or you may find yourself at the airport, sitting on your suitcase, while she's still wandering through Stuckey's, buying you chocolate coconut patties.

OPTIMUM ARRIVAL TIME is recommended between 1:00 P.M. and 3:00 P.M. This will give you the opportunity to be properly primed for the feast your mother is preparing especially for you.

Although this ground has been covered in THE ANNOUNCEMENT, she will again ask, "How long are you staying?" Whatever number of days, weeks, months, or years you respond with, you can be certain that your mother will inevitably utter what millions of mothers throughout the centuries have uttered:

IT'S SO WONDERFUL YOU'RE COMING WHAT A SHAME YOU CAN'T STAY LONGER

Preparations

For your mother, the *anticipation* of your VISIT often holds greater significance than the actual VISIT itself, expressed as

$$A > R$$

where A = anticipation and R = realization.

There are two reasons for this: first, the length of time she will spend in anticipation of your VISIT is usually greater than the length of the actual VISIT, but more importantly, your announcement creates for her an immediate call to action, a summoning of energies, a focusing of the creative spirit.

In other words, it gives her the opportunity to begin doing things

NOW!

The following are some of them:

> practicing driving the route from her home to the airport
>
> finding out if there's still a tennis court at the condo
>
> finding out if you can use the pool table at the condo
>
> finding out who's out of town just in case you need a parking space
>
> finding out if a neighbor's going to be out of town in order to have an apartment available just in case the whole family should visit at the same time (she should be so lucky!)
>
> lining up her friends for specific evenings to meet you
>
> seeing if the bottle of wine you didn't finish on your last visit is still in the refrigerator
>
> finishing off the Dolly Madison strawberry and replacing it with Haagen-Däzs chocolate-chocolate chip
>
> stocking up on pralines and coconut patties
>
> looking in the paper for free children's events
>
> seeing if the plastic floats still inflate
>
> stocking up on what she's convinced is the best suntan oil
>
> stocking up on non-diet soda

36 · How to Visit Your Mother

    stocking up on cereals other than All-Bran

    advising the condo newsletter of your visit

    stocking up on gourmet delicacies such as taco chips, Velveeta, and Ritz crackers

    putting the plastic covers on the living room furniture

    taking off the plastic covers from the living room furniture

    getting her hair done

    borrowing bridge chairs from the neighbors

    buying new plastic flowers

    buying brighter light bulbs

Obviously, in order to maximize your mother's pleasure and afford her as much time as possible in which to accomplish all the things she needs to do, we recommend you give her as much prior notice of your VISIT as possible.

The noted philosopher George Santayana once said—probably on the eve of another visit to his mother's home—

THOSE WHO CANNOT REMEMBER THE PAST ARE CONDEMNED TO REPEAT IT

Keeping this in mind, the following preparations are recommended for your forthcoming VISIT:

    pack Valium

    pack Gelusil

purchase gifts for your mother from you and the children

gather recent photos of you

gather recent photos of your kids

pack all wearable gifts your mother has given you during the last ten years

remove marijuana from your toiletry kit, pants, jackets, briefcase or pocketbook

get a haircut

pack a photo of your mother so while you're unpacking, you can tell her you never travel anywhere without it

loosen the threads on one button of your jacket or dress so you can show her you still need her help

purchase a less-revealing bathing suit than your usual one, so your mother is not embarrassed at the pool

tell your teenage daughter not to pack her diaphragm

bring the clipping from *People* saying that the ex-fiancé who left you to go live with a celebrity was just abandoned by that celebrity in favor of his boyfriend

bring a letter from your cousin telling you the aunt who swore she'd never set foot in your mother's house just fell off a chair and broke her leg

bring a news article indicating that the chemistry teacher who failed you in high school was just arrested for making LSD at night in the school lab

bring a news article indicating that the drama counselor from

Camp Kinni-Ka-Nik who insisted on painting all the kids' bodies in the musical production of *Hiawatha* was just arrested for indecent exposure

coordinate with your spouse all your secret hand signals and under-the-table nudges

bring any newspaper clipping about old enemies of your mother who are having problems with their children

More Gifts

When primitive tribes first meet, the initial interaction between the people is of utmost importance. Gift-giving rites symbolize the fact that visitors come in peace. This is as true at the airport in Fort Lauderdale as it is in the Sepik River Delta of New Guinea.

There are two types of gifts that are to be presented to your mother:

THE OFFICIAL VISIT GIFT

The Official Visit Gift should be presented only when you reach your mother's house and not before.

THE SYMBOLIC TOKEN GIFT

The Symbolic Token Gift should be presented immediately upon arrival and can be any of the following:

A HANDFUL OF EASTERN AIRLINES HANDI-WIPES

A HANDFUL OF DELTA AIRLINES SWIZZLE STICKS

AN UNUSED SET OF REPUBLIC AIRLINES PLASTIC SALT AND PEPPER SHAKERS

FOUR PACKAGES OF PAN AMERICAN SMOKED ALMONDS

THREE BOTTLES OF UNITED AIRLINES COLOGNE (one from each lavatory)

A HANDFUL OF TWA SOAPS

A HANDFUL OF AMERICAN AIRLINES SUGAR PACKETS

A HANDFUL OF WESTERN AIRLINES SWEET'N LOW PACKETS

This Token Gift-giving indicates that you have not lost your entire sense of values while living in some remote, cold corner of the United States, away from your mother.

There is one basic rule that *must* be followed with regard to The Official Visit Gift.

NEVER BRING FOOD TO YOUR MOTHER

This would be interpreted in one or all of these ways:

1. You think she can't afford to feed you.
2. You don't care for her cooking.

3. You think she lives in a primitive, remote, backward part of the world.

There are some items that you *can* bring, however. Among them are the following edible items, which your mother does not count as FOOD:

any candy that comes in a pretty packaged box is not food
(loose M&M's or halvah in a paper bag is food)

a jar of gourmet-type fruit preserves is not food
(Smucker's jelly is food)

any cookies or petits fours in a fancy tin box is not food
(a box of Mallomars or Lorna Doones is food)

assorted tins of smoked oysters in a basket with green excelsior is not food
(two whitefish in waxed paper is food)

a jar of Beluga caviar is not food
(a jar of pickled herring is food)

a bottle of Chivas Regal Scotch is not food
(a six-pack of Budweiser is food)

an assortment of French goat cheeses is not food
(Kraft American cheese slices is food)

Please bear in mind that if you bring any "non-food" food items, your opportunity to enjoy these delicacies will not arise until at least two neighbors have been shown the splendors your mother has received.

One more thought: The Official Visit Gift need not be elaborate or expensive . . . since, in effect, the real gift you are presenting your mother with on this special occasion is

YOU

THE PRE-VISIT STAGE officially ends the minute your mother spots you in the airport, train station, or bus depot. Not your spouse . . . not your children . . . YOU.

All of the fantasy and expectation, the hopes and promises of the last few weeks and days are about to be tested, as you and she enter . . .

The Visit Stage

There is only one objective during the entire time that you spend with your mother:

TO FEEL GOOD ABOUT EACH OTHER

And there is only one way by which to achieve this objective:

AVOID CONFLICT

This does not mean you can't have a good argument with your mother now and then. Of course you can.

A good argument with your mother is when whatever you are talking about, regardless of content, ends with your not taking seriously the following phrase:

AM I RIGHT?

Keeping this in mind, let us now commence the visit. In other words, your mother has just spotted you for the very first time.

Initial Contact

You should be aware that during the first sixty seconds of your mother's Initial Visual Contact with you and your family, some of the following observations will be made and conclusions drawn:

you are too fat • you are too thin • your hair is too long • your hair is too short • you're getting bald • you look tired • you look terrific • your kids are too fat • your kids are too thin • your kid's hair is too long • your kid's hair is too short • you still bite your nails • the dress you wore when you left on the last visit is the same dress you're wearing now • your hair color is too flashy • your hair color is too drab • your hair style is perfect for your face • your hair style isn't right for your face • your new eyeglasses are weird • your spouse's watch is too extravagant • you are wearing the tie she gave you last year • you're not wearing the tie she gave you this year • your pants are too tight • your dress is too tight • your skirt is too short • you're not wearing a brassiere • your daughter is not wearing a brassiere • your daughter has pink hair • your son has pink hair • you have pink hair • your daughter's wearing lipstick • your son's wearing lipstick • your son's jeans are torn and look shabby • your daughter's sneakers are worn through • your daughter is wearing only one earring • your son is wearing two earrings • your daughter had her nose done • your husband has a new toupee • your husband's toupee is too obvious • your son has nicotine stains on his fingers • your wife isn't wearing her wedding ring • your husband isn't wearing his wedding ring • your daughter is wearing a wedding ring • your daughter is wearing a nun's habit • your spouse's teeth have been straightened • you've got a gray hair • you don't have a moustache • your wife does have a moustache • your son is already shaving • you have "ring around the collar" • your daughter didn't shave her legs • the skycap noticed your teenage daughter's legs • your daughter noticed the skycap looking at her legs • something is wrong

No matter how many mental observations she makes, whether

they total twenty or two hundred, they will ALL occur within the first sixty seconds of Initial Visual Contact.

However, in spite of all the aforementioned observations and conclusions, the only comment you will hear directly from your mother is:

I'M SO HAPPY TO SEE YOU, YOU HAVE NO IDEA!

It is highly recommended that on THE RIDE from the airport, train station, or bus terminal to your mother's house—whether in her car, her neighbor's car, your rental car, a taxi, or a bus—nothing of importance be discussed. Politics, religion, or adolescent sexuality notwithstanding, there are only two important things to your mother at this moment, now that THE VISIT has commenced:

1. YOU HAVE ARRIVED
2. SHE IS WITH YOU

Any attempt to discuss any subject of more significant meaning will only lead to frustration, possible conflict, and disaster (see THE INEVITABLE BLOW-UP, page 78). Since there is nothing more important in the world at this moment than Items #1 and #2 above, and since your objective is to make THE VISIT as pleasant as possible for all concerned, you must avoid any areas of potential conflict for as long as possible.

The following topics are perfectly acceptable and advisable for discussion during the ride to your mother's home:

The Visit Stage · 47

How smooth the flight was

How the flight attendant resembled June Allyson

How Phil Donahue was on the same flight

How Marlo Thomas was *not* on the same flight

How Phil Donahue sat in coach

How your son can say the entire Gettysburg Address by heart

How hungry you are

How much you look forward to her cooking

How there's no one back home who makes [insert specialty] like she does

How green all the landscaping is here

How wonderful it is to see palm trees

Anything having to do with Barbra Streisand

How terrific Perry Como's Christmas Special was

How her golf game is doing

How her Monday night canasta group is doing

How her Thursday night canasta group is doing

What food was served at her last charity organization luncheon

The overall weather for the past two weeks here

The overall weather for the past two weeks where you live

How long your daughter held the last note of "Tomorrow" in the Talent Night at Camp Kinni-Ka-Nik

How slowly and clearly your son recited "Trees" by Joyce Kilmer

Who didn't win an Oscar and should have

Anything having to do with Ed Koch

Whether baby William resembles Prince Charles or Princess Di

How really nasty J. R. Ewing is

How great his mother, Mary Martin, was in *The Sound of Music*

How much Liza Minnelli reminds you of Judy Garland

Anything having to do with "General Hospital"

How Joan Collins' character on "Dynasty" will get hers in the end

Whatever happened to Bing Crosby's older kids

Whatever happened to Bing Crosby's wife

Whatever happened to Andy Williams' wife . . . the one who shot her boyfriend

Whatever happened to Prince Andrew's girlfriend, Koo

What kind of a name is Koo

Whether there's a Waldbaum's or a Piggly Wiggly here

How green the landscaping is in front of your mother's house

How real the flamingos look in front of your mother's house

How real the flowers look in front of your mother's house

How convenient it is to always have a parking space

How short a drive it was

Although the following topics seem to be of no great significance, they contain the potential for disaster and should absolutely be avoided:

TOPIC TO BE AVOIDED	*REASON*
airplane food	she'll think you ate already
unusually mild weather back home	she'll think you regret coming
rainy weather here	she'll think it's her fault
Mick Jagger was on the same flight	she may have no idea who he is and feel ignorant
the delay in getting your bags	she'll think it was her fault
how easy it was to get here	if it's so easy, how come you don't visit more often
how difficult it is to get here	she'll think you regret coming
an eleven-million-dollar lottery winner	she'll think you're not doing well
any comments about new construction in her area	it points out how long it's been since the last visit

how good it feels to "get away"	she'll think there's a problem back home
any mention of anyone you met during your last visit	chances are fairly good she's not talking to her or him anymore
how well Cary Grant or Bob Hope look for their age	she'll think you're trying to tell her something
any celebrity's divorce	she'll think you're trying to tell her something
the film *Snow White and The Seven Dwarfs*	she may feel guilty about how short you are; also, it depicts seven men living with a young woman
how often you and your spouse eat out	she'll think you're being extravagant or she'll think you (or your spouse) can't cook
any negative remarks about Barbra Streisand	Barbra Streisand can do no wrong
appreciation of real estate value on any home or condo except for hers	she'll think she could have made a better purchase
any mention of a pleasant conversation with anyone back home she never got along with	she'll think you've betrayed her

The Visit Stage · 51

the need to confirm your return flight	already you're thinking of going home
how much work there'll be on your desk when you return	already you're thinking of cutting short your trip
the need to call your spouse to say you've arrived safely	your mother never seems to have you to herself
any local restaurant	she'll think you want to avoid her cooking
your wife's job	she'll worry you're not doing well enough
your vasectomy	she'll think it's your wife's idea
your husband's vasectomy	she'll think he only did it to fool around
your children's allergies	she'll think they inherited them from her and it's her fault
your children's dental braces	she'll think they inherited bad teeth from her and it's her fault
your daughter got contact lenses	she'll think it's her fault
your dog just got spayed	she'll think it's her fault

summer camp for your children	why can't they spend the summer with her
getting a summer house	why can't *you* spend the summer with her

Congratulations! Now that you have had a pleasant ride from the airport, you are officially

AT HOME

Language Usage

You have just entered your mother's world—her home, her environment—and will soon mingle with her neighbors. In this world you must be prepared for differences between your language and what is spoken here.

And if you have children with you, you must constantly be prepared to translate, since much of this new language will be foreign to them.

VOCABULARY THAT YOUR MOTHER AND HER NEIGHBORS MAY USE, YOU UNDERSTAND BUT DO NOT USE, AND YOUR CHILDREN NEVER HEARD OF

dungarees
hi-fi
Victrola
hydramatic
with it
hep
mambo
beatnik
Idlewild
ukulele
The Shadow
crewcut
oleomargarine
Negro
homo
blotter
in the buff
bloomers
bebop
cellophane
tramp
galoshes
fountain pen

inkwell
pompadour
girdle
mackinaw
rain slicker
blotto
weiner
floozy
bimbo
jalopy
grip and valise
flatfoot
divorcee
futz around
backside
keester
cockamamie
necking
groovy
oilcloth
snafu
smooch

relieve yourself
alky
claptrap
malarky
femme fatale
tanked
britches
copper
chew the fat
take it on the lam
duff
starkers
slammer
in a jiffy
P.D.Q.
palooka
yap
queer
greenhorn
family jewels
hoosegow
shoot the breeze

Making a mental note of this kind of vocabulary will enable you to sit through an evening when your mother's friends come over for coffee.

VOCABULARY THAT YOU USE, YOUR CHILDREN MAY UNDERSTAND AND USE, BUT YOUR MOTHER MAY NEVER HAVE HEARD OF

mousse	video disc	it's a bummer
Beaujolais	MTV	cut-offs
Walkman	digital recording	leg warmers
floppy disk	break dance	mega-bytes
nouvelle cuisine	spaced out	wok
New Wave	fiber optics	sushi
prix fixe	open classroom	Szechuan
Adidas		

Please be aware that the use of these kinds of words in your mother's presence without any preparation may make her feel uncomfortable and "not with it." It is important that you "introduce" her to these words in a manner that doesn't make her feel as if she were the last person on earth to know about them. Even if you've been familiar with this "new thing" for years, it will feel as if you are discovering it together. Rest assured, within twenty-four hours, she will be saying to her neighbors.

THE FOLLOWING VOCABULARY CAN BE PARTICULARLY CONFUSING, SINCE THE WORDS ARE STILL BEING USED BY ALL PARTIES, BUT WITH TOTALLY DIFFERENT MEANINGS

hash	smack	pits	joint	screw	get down
coke	pansy	wired	rocker	grass	cool
drag	punk	hot	head	trash	stoned
fast	pop	fag			

COMMENTS MADE BY YOUR MOTHER WITHIN EAR-SHOT OF THE PERSON FOR WHOM IT IS INTENDED, BUT NOT ACTUALLY DIRECTED TO THAT PERSON (BY USING THIS FORM OF LANGUAGE, YOUR MOTHER ASSUMES SHE CAN EXPRESS HER THOUGHTS WITHOUT EVER BEING HELD ACCOUNTABLE)

While you're in the living room, you hear from the kitchen: WOULDN'T IT BE NICE IF SOMEONE TOOK OUT THE GARBAGE?

While standing in the supermarket check-out line, near a rather slow cashier: SOME PEOPLE JUST DON'T CARE HOW LONG THEY MAKE YOU WAIT

While you're driving your mother to the movies, a cop stops you and is looking at your license a few feet away: IT'S AMAZING HOW SOME PEOPLE ARE NEVER AROUND WHEN YOU *REALLY* NEED THEM

Getting Settled

A mere ten minutes may have elapsed since you came through the door but, with your welcoming ritual completed, your mother can now take the first step in what will be a long list of activities dedicated to

DOING-FOR-YOU

She will pose the question

ARE YOU HUNGRY?

You should not say, "I'm starved," because your mother, who is as yet still in the midst of preparing the big dinner she planned for this evening, will feel she cannot satisfy your very first need.

You should not say, "Not really," since, in doing so, you don't allow her the opportunity to DO-FOR-YOU.

Instead, the proper response, which will satisfy your mother's needs, is

I COULD EAT A LITTLE SOMETHING

This is ideal, because your mother can then happily go into the kitchen and give you just enough nourishment to Tide-You-Over while at the same time not ruin your appetite for later.

When you finish with your snack, you can proceed to unpack and get settled. To your mother this means

USING THE CLOSET

and it is the confirming gesture that indicates you are really staying.

We recommend that while you are getting settled, you present

THE OFFICIAL VISIT GIFT

which, if you have selected properly (as discussed on pages 38–41), will elicit a very pleased reaction and the inevitable statement

YOU SHOULDN'T HAVE

Very shortly thereafter, though your four-course snack is barely digested, your mother will appear in the doorway and ask you to go get ready for . . .

Dinner

No matter which evening of your visit, you will find it helpful to be aware of the following pattern: It begins with the announcement

DINNER IS READY

With everyone seated at the table, you might expect the meal to begin. You would be right. Except for one thing: there's no food on the table.

There is, on the average, anywhere from a five- to a seven-minute delay between the time you sit down and the time when the food is placed in front of you. This is because your mother

LOVES THE MOMENT

Your mother serves the food and finally you are about to dig in when you realize your mother is not at the table. From the kitchen, you hear:

START WITHOUT ME; THE FOOD'LL GET COLD

Eventually she joins you, bringing even more food. By this time, there appears to be enough food on the table to sustain Napoleon's entire army. This is due to a phenomenon known as

THE MATERNAL MULTIPLE

$$D = (M + 3) \times 4$$

Thus, if your mother knows that there will be four people, including herself, for dinner, she will go about making a roast beef for four.

In case anyone should want "seconds," this means she really should make a roast beef for eight.

In case someone isn't in the mood for beef and might wind up with nothing to eat . . . she will make some chicken as well.

But it doesn't look nice to merely put out enough chicken for only one person . . . and just in case anyone else might want some, she'll make chicken for four.

And in case everyone should want "seconds" (and if they don't want "seconds" that means they either didn't like her cooking or ate before they arrived), she needs to make enough chicken for eight.

As a result, a dinner for four will feed sixteen.

And that is why, at the end of the meal, no matter how much food is consumed, just before she's ready for the dining room table to be cleared, your mother will stand up and say:

No One Hardly Touched a Thing!

During the dinner meal you may find that the conversation is rather one-sided. This is because your mother has prepared the meal especially for you and feels that no meal is complete unless it includes sparkling

DINNER CONVERSATION

Therefore, while you are busy enjoying the benefits of her culinary skills, she will take this opportunity to conduct her very own talk show. And as the guest on this talk show, you will find your responses running the gamut from

I HAVE ABSOLUTELY NO IDEA

to

THAT'S NICE

A random sample of the kinds of statements you might encounter are as follows:

Do you ever hear from Lorraine Caminetti, that sweet girl you took to your high school prom?

I thought you'd like to know, your cousin Gwendolyn seems very happy with her third husband . . . that's what I hear anyway.

Your cousin Alfred ran into Tom Wiggens at a Proctology Convention last month in Milwaukee and Tom asked what have you been doing since the sixth grade.

How come you never call your cousin Amanda anymore?

Whatever became of Farley, that boy you brought home for Thanksgiving your freshman year in college? He was so arrogant.

Remember Mary Ellen Kilbride, that beautiful girl who lived down the street from us and who you once tried to date? Well, she's pregnant again.

Did I ever tell you that the woman who runs the magazine stand down the street says you look exactly like Richard Dreyfuss?

Remember I told you your cousin Herbie is getting married and none of us was invited? Well, it's off.

Did you ever get to watch my neighbor Ethel's son when he did the walk-on role on "Dynasty?" Well, he's been waiting on tables at some delicatessen in Los Angeles and last week he served cheesecake to Telly Savalas.

You'll never guess what else I have for dessert.

Our research indicates that conversations during the remainder of the evening touching on even the most innocent topics can often be very dangerous. Within twenty-five seconds, you can go from blissful harmony to frustrating argument with no resolution in sight, and have absolutely no idea how it happened; later that night, while lying in bed and reflecting on the evening's events, the only phrase that keeps going through your mind is

I CAN'T UNDERSTAND IT; ALL I SAID WAS . . .

it's okay for cousin Becky to share an apartment with her boyfriend Homer, even though they don't plan to get married

in today's world, a 1 A.M. Saturday curfew for a sixteen-year-old is okay with me

I think "brown" can be a color scheme for a home as well as for an office

I don't see why a sofa always has to go on the long wall

how can you say that anyone who cooks with a recipe isn't really creative

spoiling children isn't necessarily a bad thing

you know, red meat more than a couple of times a week isn't that good for you

some frozen lasagna is actually quite tasty

your neighbors seem like very nice people

You may never discover what actually caused the argument, but you must make every effort to return peace and harmony before retiring. Although you are the person who, moments before, swore you would not be able to eat anything for at least two weeks, we suggest that this is the perfect time to ask your mother what she has for

A LATE-NIGHT SNACK

Hopefully, this tactic will divert your mother's attention and bring calm to troubled waters—and a good night's sleep for all.

The First Morning

The first morning in your mother's home should, with any luck, find you rested, refreshed, and ready for a shower. As you finish your shower and turn the water off, you will then be reminded of certain House Rules that may not exist in your own home:

THE TOWELS YOU SEE ARE NOT THE TOWELS YOU USE

THE SOAPS YOU SEE ARE NOT THE SOAPS YOU USE

Although there are at least a dozen different towels of assorted sizes and colors hanging from various rings and bars, and although there are at least a dozen matching soaps of varying shapes carefully placed in soap dishes and painted sea shells throughout the bathroom, they are only there for decoration.

You should know that you, especially, are welcome to use anything in your mother's house. However, these towels and soaps were never meant to be touched by human hands.

Your towel is to be found in the cabinet under the sink, at least six feet away from the shower.

And the soap you were supposed to have just used can be found stacked in the corner of the medicine cabinet, above the sink.

While your mother is preparing breakfast in the kitchen, you may wander around the house with a cup of coffee in your hand. In doing so, you will become readily reminded that in addition to being Your Mother, she is also the Director of

THE SOCIETY FOR THE PRESERVATION OF ABSOLUTELY EVERYTHING WITH REGARD TO YOUR LIFE:

- your hospital baby bracelet
- a photo of you getting your first haircut
- a photo of you sitting on a pony
- your bronzed baby shoes
- a photo of you pinning an orchid corsage on your mother at your elementary school graduation
- a photo of you in a cap and gown at your high school graduation
- a photo of the cast and crew of your senior class production of *Our Town*
- a photo of the family around a table when cousin Gwendolyn got married the first time
- a picture of you in your first white dinner jacket, dancing with Lorraine Caminetti at your senior prom
- three leather bookmarks you made at Camp Kinni-Ka-Nik
- a box-stitched plastic lanyard with the whistle you

used when you became waterfront counselor at Camp Kinni-Ka-Nik
- a picture of you dressed as a wolf, standing next to Suzie Fidler dressed as Little Red Riding Hood at the Broad Channel Day Camp Carnival
- a close-up photo of the trout you caught one summer at your family's cabin at Lake Shawanga
- a picture of you standing in front of the Eiffel Tower
- a certificate for being runner-up in a spelling bee
- a photo of the entire family at your parents' twentieth anniversary party in a Holiday Inn
- a photo of you in a pair of red hot-pants at a Fourth of July picnic
- a picture of you and your children standing next to a mule at the Grand Canyon
- your official wedding picture
- a picture of you and cousin Gwendolyn in Acapulco
- a photo of some of the family on top of a mountain when cousin Gwendolyn got married the second time
- a photo of you and all your girlfriends doing the Bunny Hop at your sweet sixteen party
- a picture of you feeding your child cake at his first birthday party
- a photo of your daughter dancing with both your parents at their fortieth wedding anniversary party
- a photo of your son on the Camp Kinni-Ka-Nik Recreation Hall stage, framed along with his letter to you saying, "Thanks for sending the tap shoes; I was the best one on Talent Night!"

Planning a Day's Activities

Planning a day's activities, no matter what day of your visit, is always done at the breakfast table.

When you arrive at the breakfast table, you will notice immediately that

THERE'S NOT ONE PATCH OF EMPTY SPACE VISIBLE

This is because breakfast at your mother's is a one-course meal, consisting of everything that's in the refrigerator except for what was left over from last night's meal. And in spite of the array of edibles set before you, your mother will then stand next to you and say

SO WHAT CAN I MAKE YOU FOR BREAKFAST

The answer to this question is almost irrelevant. Not only do you have enough on the table for 3.1 meals, if you indicate that you don't really want eggs, she'll probably respond with

I'LL MAKE THEM ANYWAY; SOMEONE'LL EAT THEM

While sitting at your place, you will also notice that your mother has arranged all the food platters as if she had designed her own version of the videogame Space Invaders. If you empty a dish, another full one immediately takes its place. And the faster you eat, the faster they come.

As you finish the last morsel of eggs (which you hadn't wanted in the first place), you can be sure that your mother will ask

SO WHAT WOULD YOU LIKE FOR LUNCH

Our research indicates that no matter what you decide on, it will be accompanied by almost everything that's now going back into the refrigerator.

At about this time, your mother will inquire as to what you'd like to do for the rest of the day. Please bear in mind that although it *sounds* as if you have the whole day, part of it will be taken up with accompanying her to

The Mall

Going shopping with your mother is not merely an activity to restock her cupboard and refrigerator. It is an opportunity to show you that anything and everything you may have available to you back home is *also* available where *she* lives.

We are sure you can probably come up with a couple of items that are *not* available in your mother's locale.

We recommend that you not mention them.

If you think your mother knows her way around her own home, just watch her maneuver through the supermarket at her favorite mall. As you push the shopping cart, your mother will proudly lead the way, guiding you past countless islands of this mercantile archipelago. And like an Indian guide leading a naive explorer through unchartered waters, she will take great pleasure in pointing out all that lies before you. Please understand that although there may be 5,792 different items available, your mother is in the habit of buying no more than 40 of them. However, she takes great pride in pointing out to you the other 5,752 items since, as far as she is concerned,

THEY'RE ALWAYS THERE IF I WANT THEM

There's another reason why you are going shopping with your mother: She wants you to know that

IF HER SHOPPING MALL WERE THE SUPERBOWL, SHE'D BE THE STAR QUARTERBACK

And this is her big moment to introduce you to the other members of her All-Star Team.

As a result, when you approach the meat department, she will point out her very own butcher, Rudy, an artist whose medium is veal, who gives new meaning to the word "lean," and who has a wonderful wife formerly of Akron, a good-looking son who goes to some college in North Carolina, and a sixteen-year-old daughter who only gives him grief.

After introducing you to him, you will then move on to the delicatessen area where Sal will not only wax eloquent on the glories of his potato salad, pepperoni, and fresh mozzarella but, only because it's your mother, will give you a taste of everything in his showcase. While you are nibbling away and your mother is pointing out the best part of the smoked salmon from which to slice, she will inquire as to the health of Sal's wife, Angelina (who's a beautician), his son Anthony (who's studying for the priesthood), his other son Sal, Jr. (who's an accountant), and Angelina's mother (who's been living with them for the past fifteen years).

Finally, you will be introduced to Gladys in fruits and vegetables, who, as far as your mother is concerned, has a nose for freshness that is unequaled. Gladys will take your mother aside and, under her breath, warn her to stay away from the eggplant. In gratitude, your mother will buy twice as many cucumbers as she needs, even though she knows they give her gas.

The fruit and vegetable department is your opportunity to acknowledge the true expertise of your mother.

We recommend your reaching for the nearest cantaloupe on the stand, feeling it briefly, and then handing it to your mother, saying

WHAT DO YOU THINK OF THIS ONE, MOM?

This will give your mother the opportunity to show you the bruise on the opposite side, tell you it's over-ripe, and announce that it will not be sweet. Passing it casually to Gladys the Nose, your mother will immediately dip into the pile and come up with a winner, causing Gladys to remark

NOW, THAT'S A CANTALOUPE!

Now that you understand why part of your day will be taken up with accompanying your mother on the shopping trip, you are better equipped to plan the rest of the day's activities.

Your mother is eager to offer a list of daytime and evening activities and places to visit in her area.

We strongly recommend that you listen to ALL her suggestions before reacting to any ONE:

- ○ the Sleepydale High School production of *The Best of Chekhov*
- ○ the Crestwood Community Theater production of *Medea*
- ○ the Second Annual Firemen's Hot Chili Cook-off
- ○ the Polynesian Revue at the Club Mai-Tai
- ○ the International Challenge Cup Croquet Finals
- ○ Pamela Peacock and The Little Big Band at Don's Steak House
- ○ Mark Twain's Dixieland Revue at the Musicana Dinner Theatre
- ○ the Roaring Twenties Night at Poinciana Place
- ○ the Official State Preliminary for the National Little Miss Pageant at the Phoenix Holiday Inn
- ○ the Spring Fashion Show sponsored by the Dream Faces Modelling Agency at the Twin Cities Mall
- ○ a lively exhibition of Japanese woodblock prints at the Morikami Museum
- ○ "An Evening With Dante, the Eternal Poet," at the Centro di Studi Italiani
- ○ a "Name the Hotel Dining Room" contest at the Sunshine Valley Motor Lodge
- ○ a display of Amish quilts at the Daughters of the American Revolution Auditorium
- ○ a fish fry at the Veterans of Foreign Wars

- a "Crafts and Ice Sculpture Show" on the patio of the Palmetto Park Hotel (come early)
- the Annual Country-and-Western Jamboree, starring Billie-Mae Dallas and the Sea Turtle Cloggers at Whispering Pines Park (bring your own ribs and chicken, folding chairs and beach blanket)
- a tour of the Cypress Swamp Boardwalk, given by the U.S. Fish and Wildlife Service
- a white-belt karate demonstration by youngsters six through eleven at Mrs. Boynton's Day School
- Mirabella Swann giving an organ recital at the Mesa Verde Chapel, using the magnificent 90 Rank Austin pipe organ
- an auction of antique napkin rings at Rita's Shawnee Avenue Gallery
- a tour through the Lion Country Safari Theme Park and Camp Ground
- an afternoon jam session at Harpoon Louie's
- a Buffet Luncheon Cruise on the "La Notte" glass bottom boat, which sails from Phil Foster Park
- a day-trip to the Rutledge Park Zoo to see the world-famous Marching Flamingos
- Roger Brown's World of Miniature Horses
- a tour of the Lovin' Oven Bakery with free samples

Whatever activities you select, we strongly recommend that they include your mother whenever possible. After all, you must not forget that you are there for THE VISIT.

If your mother happens to live in a Sun Belt area, and has access to a pool, she will be more than delighted if you pass up her list, since it will then give her the opportunity to spend the day showing you off at *the pool.*

The Pool

In your mother's community the pool area is often the forum where information is exchanged, where new acquisitions are displayed, and where children's forthcoming visits are heralded. It is also the place where, no matter how many times you have visited, you will make your

OFFICIAL PUBLIC DEBUT

To enable you to get through a day at the pool, we offer the following advice:

READING MATERIAL—We recommend light reading such as one-panel cartoon books. Throughout the course of the day your mother will be introducing you to a steady stream of friends and acquaintances and as a result, there is no way you can concentrate on anything that requires more continuity than a cartoon caption.

WEARING APPAREL—String bikinis and French scuba divers' briefs are perfectly marvelous for the pool area . . . as long as they are on someone who's not related to your mother.

Your mother may insist on your wearing a T-shirt to the pool area because she "knows the sun and you don't." Do not wear one that says "I feel no pain with cocaine."

Be aware that although you may be most comfortable wearing your torn, faded, and softest beach shirt, your favorite for the past ten years, anything in such shabby condition worn by you within fifty feet of your mother is going to be a reflection on *her*. We recommend you wear, once again, the aquamarine beach jacket dotted with yellow sailfish that your mother bought you during your last visit and that you "forgot" to pack when you left.

MISCELLANEOUS POOLSIDE ADVICE:

Use only the suntan oil your mother gives you. Even though you're perfectly satisfied with the lotion you've been using for years, you spent too much for it and what do the French know anyway about sun.

Do not take offense when your mother tells you you're not allowed to splash, run, or make noise. By now it should be no surprise to you . . . even though she's telling you this while you're sitting quietly on your beach chair reading *The Wall Street Journal*.

Smile and be gracious when your mother introduces you to a neighbor whose son, Buddy, sells life insurance near where you live and who told his mother he can't wait to meet you.

Do not say, "Are you kidding?" to the three people your mother has introduced you to that day, each of whom has said, "Ahhh, it's a shame you can't stay longer."

Finally, although you may happen to spot certain people whom you met on previous visits, do not attempt to acknowledge any of them until your mother says it's okay. You will know exactly what the status of their relationship is if you say to your mother, "Isn't that Mrs. Hufnagle over there?" and with eyes still riveted on the newspaper article she's reading, she responds with

Dining Out

The day will come during the course of your VISIT when you will eat out at a restaurant. This is not the same as if you were to go to a restaurant back home with your spouse or friends.

To begin with, restaurants in your mother's area are extensions of her turf. Although she does not own any restaurants, she acts as if she has a proprietary interest in some of them.

The selection of where to eat, as far as your mother is concerned, is based on a number of criteria:

1. HOW MANY PEOPLE SHE KNOWS WILL SEE YOU THERE TOGETHER
2. HOW LARGE THE PORTIONS ARE
3. IF THE MAITRE D' SMILES, GIVES HER A WINK, AND SAYS, "HOW NICE TO SEE YOU *AGAIN*"
4. IF THE ARRAY OF ITEMS ON THE SALAD BAR MAKES HER BELIEVE THAT SHE CAN PUT TOGETHER A WHOLE MEAL FROM THOSE ITEMS ALONE
5. IF THE WAITRESS ALWAYS MANAGES TO HUNT DOWN TWO EXTRA PUMPERNICKEL ROLLS
6. IF SHE DOESN'T LIKE WHAT SHE ORDERED, THE WAITRESS OFFERS TO BRING HER SOMETHING ELSE . . . AND NOT CHARGE HER
7. IF THERE'S ALWAYS A PARKING SPACE
8. IF YOU DON'T HAVE TO MAKE RESERVATIONS
9. IF THE BARTENDER MAKES HER SLOE GIN FIZZ WITH JUST THE RIGHT AMOUNT OF FIZZ
10. IF THEY GIVE HER A DOGGIE BAG WITHOUT HER EVEN ASKING
11. IF THERE'S AN "EARLY-BIRD SPECIAL"

Although these eleven criteria are important to your mother, there's probably nothing more important in selecting a restaurant than the value she receives for her money. Nothing bears this out more than her ability to seek out specific restaurants on special nights when they offer

ALL YOU CAN EAT

Many of these restaurants may, in fact, have such ordinary food that your mother wouldn't even think of eating there on a normal evening. However, the lure of incredible value for her dollar, coupled with the opportunity to feed you unlimited amounts, is too hard to pass up.

As a result, if it's Tuesday and you're really looking forward to ribs, you'd better start thinking shrimp.

One more recommendation: As your meal draws to a close, you may witness your mother engaged in conversation with the manager of the restaurant . . . who firmly but politely is saying to her

I'M SORRY, MADAM, BUT ON ALL-YOU-CAN-EAT NIGHTS WE SIMPLY DO NOT GIVE OUT DOGGIE BAGS

Just drop your car keys under the table, get down on all fours, and proceed to look for them until the conversation is over.

Sooner or later, often because THE VISIT is drawing to a close, our research indicates that you may encounter shifts in mood and temperament while engaged in various activities with your mother. These shifts signal the beginning of . . .

The Inevitable Blow-Up

For whatever reason, and the reasons may be as varied as there are mothers, some innocuous remark or situation will serve as a reminder of some dormant thought floating around in her mind. The precipitating remark or situation may have nothing whatsoever to do with you and, in fact, you may not even be present when it occurs. But it almost doesn't matter . . . since you will experience the result of it very soon thereafter.

Here are some examples:

a neighbor remarks on the high cost of new dentures	YOU SHOULD HAVE BECOME A DENTIST LIKE SHE REALLY WANTED YOU TO
she sees a freckle-faced four-year-old in a cereal commercial	WHO ARE YOU TO DECIDE NOT TO HAVE CHILDREN
a billboard announces a "Grandmother's Day" at the Children's Zoo, two days after you're scheduled to leave	JUST BECAUSE *YOU* HAVE TO GET BACK IS NO REASON WHY YOUR CHILDREN CAN'T STAY AN EXTRA WEEK

she heard the unemployment rate rose 2 percent last month	WHY DID YOU GIVE UP TEACHING WHEN YOU ONLY HAD TEN MORE YEARS TILL RETIREMENT
she reads that a Picasso was just sold for $3,000,000 in an auction	HOW COULD YOU PUT THAT SOFA-SIZE ORIGINAL OIL PAINTING OF *NOAH'S ARK* SHE GAVE YOU IN STORAGE
Rudy the butcher tells her he thinks real estate values are on the way down	WHAT'S SO GREAT ABOUT THE SUBURBS THAT YOU'VE DECIDED TO MOVE THERE
she reads in *People* that Phil Donahue bought a home in the suburbs	YOU'VE MADE SUCH A NICE LIFE FOR YOURSELF IN THE SUBURBS, WHY WOULD YOU DECIDE TO MOVE BACK TO THE CITY
she sees a rerun of "The Newlywed Game"	YOU ARE STAYING SINGLE JUST TO GET EVEN WITH HER
your eight-year-old announces at the pool that the Children's Zoo sucks	HOW CAN YOU RAISE YOUR CHILDREN TO BE SO RUDE

your ten-year-old asks you for a quarter to play a video game and you give it to him	HOW CAN YOU LET YOUR CHILDREN SPEND MONEY LIKE IT GROWS ON TREES

These thoughts will never be verbalized at the time they occur to her. This is because she is trying her best to avoid head-on confrontation during your visit.

However, just like in the *Tarzan* movies when the jungle suddenly turns strangely silent, the atmosphere begins to be charged. You will know that this phenomenon is taking place when you ask your mother if there's anything wrong and receive the following answer:

WRONG? WHY SHOULD ANYTHING BE WRONG?

This is your first indication that something is *definitely* wrong. But our research indicates there is little you can do about it, since whatever may be bothering your mother will only be disclosed when she decides

IT'S TIME

As the "time" nears, your mother will reach the point where she can contain herself no longer and, just when you casually remark that there's no more orange juice in the refrigerator, she will exclaim

MAYBE YOUR *NEXT* MOTHER WILL DO A BETTER JOB!

which might prompt you to say

"WHAT'S THAT SUPPOSED TO MEAN?"

giving the green light to your mother, who will then say

YOU DON'T KNOW WHAT THAT MEANS? OKAY, SINCE YOU ASKED, I'LL *TELL* YOU!

A statement such as this one is the indicator that THE INEVITABLE BLOW-UP has arrived. Within seconds, the floodgates are opened and a torrent of grievances, many of which you thought had long since been resolved, come rushing at you. This is why, for no apparent reason you suddenly find yourself having to deal with a situation such as:

> when your eight-year-old son was born, you named him after your *spouse's* father
>
> OR
>
> she has never once seen you use the wedding gift she gave you
>
> OR
>
> when your fourteen-year-old daughter was born, you called your mother-in-law first

Our research indicates that during the course of THE INEVITABLE BLOW-UP there is absolutely nothing you can say or do to calm the waters. This is not the time to tell her a funny story or to play Streisand singing "The Way We Were."

Even a simple "But Mom . . ." will only aggravate the situation.

We strongly recommend this course of action:

KEEPING YOUR MOUTH SHUT

We also recommend that you look at the nearest calendar and make a mental note of the amount of time left before your departure. This is because the most important factor in resolving The Inevitable Blow-Up is

TIMING

Many people feel that the best way to resolve The Inevitable Blow-Up is to arbitrarily apologize for any of the supposed wrongs. This is not advisable. What *is* advisable is to indicate that you're sorry she's upset.

The only element that will then help reestablish peaceful coexistence is TIME. If you understand that no matter what you say, these grievances may never be resolved, and you understand that your mother's *feelings* are genuine (even though the facts may be *another* story), it is merely a question of waiting it out.

Which is why we recommend your looking at the calendar and making a mental note of your departure date. In the interest of future relations

YOU DO NOT WANT TO LEAVE WITHOUT RESOLVING THE BLOW-UP

If the Blow-Up occurs Thursday night and you're leaving on Sunday, TIME is on your side. If it occurs Thursday night and you're leaving Friday morning

YOU'VE GOT A PROBLEM

The only thing we recommend is to put on the aquamarine beach jacket with the yellow sailfish, and throw yourself on the mercy of the court, saying in as calm a voice as possible, "We only have a few more hours together; let's not let it ruin the whole visit."

Assuming The Inevitable Blow-Up has been resolved and the grievances have been relegated to a state of DETENTE BUT NOT FORGOTTEN, you are ready to begin the most delicate part of your VISIT:

The Departure

Since your mother is as aware as you are of exactly when you will be leaving, no mention should be made of departure nor should you begin packing *anything* until after dinner on the night before. To do so earlier would be considered cruel and inhuman punishment. If you need to reconfirm your return reservation on the phone, do it in another room, out of earshot. Your mother is very sensitive about this, and nowhere is this better demonstrated than in her kitchen, forty-eight hours prior to your departure. It is at this time she realizes

THERE ARE ONLY SIX MORE MEALS TO GO

We recommend that during this crucial countdown you be particularly sympathetic and understanding. As a result of the limited amount of time left to THE VISIT, the choice of which activity to do or what to eat takes on greater importance. For example, the argument *for* playing tennis the last day of your VISIT is that you can always use a little extra relaxation before returning to your normally hectic schedule. The argument *against* playing tennis the last day of your VISIT is that you've had plenty of relaxation and your mother would really like you to join her at the auction of antique napkin rings at Rita's Shawnee Avenue Gallery.

We recommend that the choice you make be determined solely on the basis of what activities keep you and your mother together for the entire day. There are two reasons for this: Because she is so aware that you will be leaving shortly, any time spent away from her may be interpreted as your not *wanting* to be with her. Secondly, by spending the last day with her, you will be leaving her with as positive a remembrance of your visit as possible.

The last dinner she makes also assumes special significance. Whereas she herself made all the selections for your Arrival Dinner, she will now give YOU the opportunity to choose anything you desire . . . as long as it provides her with the chance to once again demonstrate her skill in the kitchen.

Although the things you love to eat might run the gamut from lobster to linguini, the most important criterion your mother will apply in helping you choose what she prepares will always be

CAN YOU TAKE SOME WITH YOU WHEN YOU GO

If you think breakfast the *first* morning of your VISIT was sumptuous, it doesn't even compare to what your mother lays out the morning you depart. Your mother does this, secure in the knowledge that you will not eat nearly as well again until the next time you visit.

LEAVING YOUR MOTHER'S can be an extraordinarily frustrating and difficult experience for you, unless you are aware of exactly what's happening. And what's happening is an unconscious effort on your mother's part to

PROLONG YOUR VISIT

This will take various forms:

>she resets the alarm clock before it rings, just to give you "an extra ten minutes"
>
>she offers a greater assortment of breakfast choices, which require longer preparation and clean-up time
>
>she decides that this is the best time to sort out the frayed pot-holders from the good ones
>
>she discovers that the fruit-shaped magnets which hold the "Don't Forget" memos, recipes, and your child's drawings on the refrigerator door all need rearranging
>
>she begins to assemble your traveling Care Package, which will contain the remains of last night's dinner plus enough food to nourish you comfortably should you happen to be marooned on a desert island for a week
>
>she decides that this is the best time to clean out the toaster
>
>upon seeing your suitcase emerging from your room, she suddenly remembers at least four "gifts" she had intended to give you, and disappears to look for them
>
>she writes down all twenty-one ingredients of the dessert you seemed to like so much the night before

With no knowledge of what is happening, you would probably be tearing your hair out at this point, looking at your watch, and wondering how on earth you're still going to make your travel connection. We recommend that you add at least one extra hour to any normal departure time you think you might need. This will allow you to calmly put your bags in the car or a taxi or whatever you are taking to make your connection, while your mother plays out the departure ritual.

If you are taking your mother's car to the airport, we strongly recommend that *you* drive. If your mother drives, a number of things might happen:

she might try an entirely new route she heard about from Rudy the butcher

she might stop to get the car washed

she decides to stop for gas, even though she filled up yesterday morning

when she decides to stop "just for gas," she will ask the mechanic to come over and listen to the knock in the engine that you know has been there for at least six months

she expresses concern that she might have left her front door unlocked and wants to telephone a neighbor about it

the closer she gets to your travel connection, the slower the car will seem to go

We recommend that when you finally arrive at your travel connection, you thank your mother profusely, kiss her goodbye, and disappear. This is because at this point it should be very clear to both of you that you are in fact leaving . . . and any unplanned-for delays with your travel connection might give her false hope that you may stay longer.

You and your mother are about to part and you are both pleased that you had a successful time together. Even so, do not be surprised when you pick up your suitcase and turn to go that she will look at you and say tenderly

IT WAS WONDERFUL TO SEE YOU
WHAT A SHAME YOU COULDN'T STAY LONGER

If you think that THE VISIT is now over and THE POST-VISIT STAGE has begun, you are mistaken. As far as your mother is concerned

JUST BECAUSE YOU'VE SAID GOODBYE DOESN'T
MEAN YOU'VE LEFT

The Post-Visit Stage

The POST-VISIT STAGE officially begins the moment your mother knows that you've arrived safely. This behavior hearkens back to those days when she waited up for you to return home while you were out with your friends. The familiar sound of your key in the door was her assurance that all was well, and even though you are now considerably older, that comfort factor for her is still needed.

We recommend that you telephone upon your arrival and let her know you're okay. (You could conceivably drop her a postcard or a letter rather than call, but this only means she will have to worry a lot longer.)

When you call, thank her for a wonderful VISIT. Keep the conversation short and, above all, bear in mind the fact that any adversity you might have experienced on your trip back will still be considered by your mother as part of the VISIT and she'll feel responsible. After all, if you hadn't come to visit her, it wouldn't have happened in the first place. Therefore, we recommend you heed the following advice:

do not mention how much you had to pay for excess baggage as a result of all her "gifts"

do not mention that after you kissed her goodbye, you then sat for an hour in the station because your train was late

do not mention if your flight was bumpy or the bus broke down on the way home

do not even think of mentioning that you ate the meal on the plane

if you unfortunately wound up sitting across from Mrs. Hufnagle, tell your mother you successfully avoided having any conversation with her

do not mention that you had one martini in the airport before you left, and then three more on the flight

do not mention that the person next to you had also just visited her mother and also had three martinis

tell her that the flight attendant had never before seen a dinner for twelve packed so well that it fit perfectly under the seat in front of you

do not mention that the plastic container your mother sealed so well opened up, and that according to the flight crew, no matter what they do, the plane's going to smell from marinara sauce for at least two weeks

CONGRATULATIONS!

Once you have made this phone call, you have officially entered

THE POST-VISIT STAGE

Within four days we recommend that you once again telephone your mother to solidify the fact that you had

A WONDERFUL VISIT

In discussing how wonderful THE VISIT was, you cannot shower too many compliments on her. However, we caution you not to single out any one person, place, or meal as being outstanding, since your mother may interpret this to mean you didn't like all the others. The only person who you *should* single out is your mother and the only meals you should talk about are the Arrival Meal and the Last Dinner.

The *most* important reason for placing this SECOND FOLLOW-UP CALL is that it may help you find out what your mother *really* thought of THE VISIT. She has had a few days to relax and contemplate the entire VISIT and if there's anything that bothers her, she will either tell you directly in this phone call or you will discern it in her tone of voice. If you have followed all the advice in this Manual, you will be pleased to hear how much THE VISIT meant to her, and can hang up, content in that knowledge.

We can tell you with certainty that you have successfully come full circle, and you are once again entering THE PRE-VISIT STAGE, since the moment your mother hangs up, she will realize

      1. You're not with her *right now*
      2. You haven't *just been* with her

which (as you should have learned by now) can mean only one thing in your mother's mind:

SO WHEN ARE YOU COMING TO SEE ME?